SKILLS FOR SUCCESS™

STRENGTHENING PUBLIC SPEAKING SKILLS

DON RAUF

Rosen
YA™

New York

Published in 2018 by The Rosen Publishing Group, Inc.
29 East 21st Street, New York, NY 10010

First Edition

Library of Congress Cataloging-in-Publication Data

Names: Rauf, Don, author.
Title: Strengthening public speaking skills / Don Rauf.
Description: New York : Rosen Publishing, 2018. | Series: Skills for success | Includes bibliographical references and index. | Audience: Grade 7–12.
Identifiers: ISBN 9781508175704 (library bound)
Subjects: LCSH: Public speaking—Juvenile literature. | Speechwriting—Juvenile literature.
Classification: LCC PN4129.15 R38 2018 | DDC 808.5'1—dc23

Manufactured in the United States of America

CONTENTS

INTRODUCTION

For many people, the idea of speaking in front of a crowd fills them with dread. The fear of speaking in public is so common in fact that it even has its own medical term—glossophobia. The thought of presenting oneself before a group of people can certainly be nerve-wracking. Learning to communicate before an audience, however, can help individuals succeed throughout their lives. With practice, the fear can be overcome. And even if a person does not have the natural ability to give a stirring talk, he or she can take steps to develop the talent and become a good public speaker.

Billionaire businessman Richard Branson certainly knows the power of strong communication skills. On his blog, Branson quotes business author Brian Tracy: "Communication is a skill that you can learn. It's like riding a bicycle or typing. If you're willing to work at it, you can rapidly improve the quality of every part of your life."

Entrepreneur Elon Musk proves the point. An article in *Forbes* online describes how Musk is not a naturally extroverted person and was a horrendous speaker who would shake with anxiety. With time and practice, however, he has "learned not to do that." Now he gives many

Even in a high-tech world where online communication may dominate, public speaking is a powerful "low-tech" skill that can influence, inform, and inspire.

presentations about his business ventures and his visions for the future—including a manned mission to Mars.

In this high-tech world, it may seem surprising that the very low-tech skill of public speaking still carries such great power. A good public speaker informs, directs, and inspires. He or she can influence employees, bosses, and coworkers. Because public speaking is often key to motivating people and demonstrating strength and character, it is usually essential for anyone in a leadership role. The process of putting together a talk also helps the presenter to develop a point of view. For some, stepping behind a mic can be a step toward overcoming a fear of failure. In the long run, the mastery of public speaking can advance individuals in the classroom and at work.

While people have to seek out opportunities to talk in front of a group, they may be surprised at the number of times they have actually already tried public speaking but have not realized it. They probably have expressed ideas in front of a classroom or to a group of friends. They may have said a few words to a gathering at a birthday party. They may have already spoken at a meeting. Even if they have told a tale at the dinner table, that's a little step toward public speaking. These experiences can be the very first building blocks for talking in front of larger audiences. The more you take advantage of opportunities to communicate with others verbally, the better and more confident you will become. In fact, you may find that you're good at it, and it could even be fun.

Why Speak in Public?

Talking in front of a crowd is a powerful skill that has been used throughout history and continues to this day. Just think how important public speaking skills are for political candidates and leaders. Or search online for the ideas organization TED Talks and the impact its presentations have been having on the world. This nonprofit is devoted to spreading ideas by having experts give speeches. Every day 450,000 people log on to view a range of presentations that are available from this organization, according to TED.com. Themes range from "What Makes You Happy?" to "How to Be a Great Leader." In this day and age of flashy videos and slick movies, the power of the spoken word—without any special effects—can still have a great impact.

SPREADING THE WORD

When you need to inform a group about upcoming events, work that needs to be done, or how things are going in a business or group, public speaking can be an efficient way to educate an audience about a topic. An informational speech can take on many different forms. It can explain the meaning, theory, or philosophy of a topic. If you were a teacher lecturing on democracy or free speech, you'd have to define what they are to your class. An informative speech can accomplish this. It can also demonstrate how something works—like the game of Ping-Pong or the gears on a ten-speed bike or a microwave oven. When Apple unveils a new version of the iPhone, the company executives explain the latest model before a packed auditorium.

Having an interesting subject matter can make all the difference in whether a speech is a hit or not. To help its students who may have to make a speech for a communications class or another course, Austin Community College offers students a list of informative speech topics that it thinks would grab the attention of listeners and "tickle the imagination." The topics include the use of human cadavers, women in the military, the reality show phenomenon, and tsunamis. The list is very diverse, but it's meant to be inspiring. It is designed to get students thinking creatively about possible subjects they might like to discuss.

Visual aids can certainly help, too. If you were explaining how to get honey from bees, you might not only show photos of bees and a honey harvest but also bring in a frame from a beehive and show how bees build their honeycomb and store the honey.

Public speakers need to engage their audiences. They may do this by asking questions, using visual aids, and making sure that their topic is interesting.

When explaining how to do something in a speech, you might use a step-by-step approach, often numbering the steps as you go—whether it is for making a home-made music video for YouTube, handling the college application process, or completing some other task.

Sometimes, your goal in an informative speech may be to explain how something happened or will happen. Posing a question or puzzle to a crowd can intrigue them and get them thinking. How will the school cafeteria be changing the food it serves? How did dinosaurs possibly go extinct? Vivid descriptions can bring the topic to life—some say a gigantic meteor crashed to Earth or ash and gas spewing from volcanoes left dinosaurs gasping for air and finally killed them. To make a memorable speech, create a vivid picture in the listeners' minds.

SPEECHES THAT MADE A DIFFERENCE

Throughout history, public speeches have affected the course of world events. Sometimes, the spoken word can be the most powerful force in the world, changing the way many people act and think. Here are a few examples.

- **Martin Luther King Jr.'s "I Have a Dream" Speech.** On August 28, 1963, during the March on Washington for Jobs and Freedom, the civil rights leader Martin Luther King Jr. spoke before a crowd of 250,000 at the Lincoln Memorial in Washington, DC. He described his dream for the United States as a place of racial equality. His words resonated with the masses and spurred a movement for equal rights, culminating ultimately with the passage of the Civil Rights Act of 1964, which outlawed discrimination based on race, color, religion, sex, or national origin.

- **John F. Kennedy's Inaugural Address.** When John F. Kennedy was sworn in as the thirty-fifth president of the United States on January 20, 1961, his speech inspired people to be less self-serving and devote their energies to making the United States a better place. His line "Ask not what your country can do for you—ask what you can do for your country" motivated thousands of young Americans to pursue public service. On NPR, Gonzalo Barrientos, who was a freshman at the University of Texas at the time said of the speech, "He spoke for all of us, he spoke to all of us whether you were poor, rich, whatever color, whatever background as an American—that was especially inspiring to me."

- **Franklin Delano Roosevelt's First Inaugural Address.** Franklin Roosevelt said the famous words "The only thing we have to fear is fear itself" as part of his inaugural address on March 4, 1933, when he became the thirty-second president of the United States. At the time, the country was in the middle of the Great Depression, an epic economic crisis. By 1933, some 13 to 15 million Americans were unemployed and nearly half of the country's banks had failed. His speech gave confidence and comfort to a nation that was struggling to get back on its feet, and Americans moved on from that point with a new spirit.

WE CAN WORK IT OUT

"Try to see it my way. Do I have to keep on talking 'till I can't go on?" These lyrics from the Beatles song "We Can Work It Out" capture one possible purpose for making a presentation: to convince an audience to see your point of view. Students often have opportunities to practice the power of persuasive speaking with their parents because they're often trying to convince parents to get the things they want—to have a sleepover with friends, to borrow the car, or to get concert tickets.

To persuade parents, young people need to show the

While a good speech will hold a crowd's attention, a truly effective presentation will spur people to take action. A persuasive talk can get a group to agree with the speaker's point of view.

rationale for their argument and show how their proposal benefits their audience (the parents). The young person may say, "I will continue to get good grades, mow the lawn, and keep my room clean, but in return I would appreciate having a few friends over for a sleepover on a Friday night." Many who speak before an assembled group are trying to reach a similar goal—to influence and convince people to see things their way.

An effective public speech has this power to persuade. If you deliver your position with conviction and passion, you can convince people to take action. A strong speech may help a politician gain support in an election or motivate individuals to contribute funds to a worthy cause. On the University of Pittsburgh website, a section about teaching oral communication stresses how persuasive speaking involves having a sense of your audience. You have to meet them halfway. Most audiences will have some who agree with you, some who disagree, and some who are undecided. It can be almost impossible to bring those who disagree with you to your side, so directing your thoughts to those who are undecided can often be the best approach.

To convince others to see it your way, you need to understand the concerns of the undecided listeners and be able to address those concerns with facts. Also, in your arsenal for persuasion consider using statistics, quotations, humor, personal stories, and research. Being passionate about your point of view can also sway a crowd.

You may have very specific goals in your persuasive

speech—wanting people to donate money, sign a petition, vote for a cause, or write to a government representative. In a school setting, a student might be encouraging other students to give to a canned food drive at Thanksgiving. The student may ask people in the audience to tell what they eat on Thanksgiving—turkey, mashed potatoes, cranberry sauce, stuffing, and so on. This gets them thinking about how lucky they are to have such good food. And then the speaker may explain how some poorer families in the neighborhood have only a can of soup for dinner or nothing at all at Thanksgiving.

Presenting a real-life story about a family struggling to put food on the table can have a great impact. Appealing to people's good nature can make a difference and they may be more likely to donate. Explaining how they might feel good contributing could help the cause. Listeners may agree with a point you present, but a truly effective speech gets people to take action.

THAT'S ENTERTAINMENT

Sometimes a public speech is more about keeping people amused than anything else. A talk may be before an audience in a theater or to honor someone on his or her birthday. Monologues, which are another type of public speaking, are hugely popular today. Check out the program *The Moth* on National Public Radio—it features people telling their personal stories, usually before a live

Don't underestimate the power of humor. If you can get an audience to laugh, you can win them over.

audience. Or even listen to a favorite comedian. In most cases, humor is an effective way to connect with an audience, and it boosts the energy level in a room.

A funny opening line, such as "If you can't hear me, please raise your hand," can warm up an audience and win them over right from the start. Comical quotes from famous people might be used, depending on the occasion. And self-deprecating humor can work, too, as long as it doesn't go overboard.

CHAPTER TWO

How to Build an Amazing Speech

Before you step before a crowd and wow them with your presentation, you need to write out your speech. Although you may have a topic or a basic idea to discuss, the process of building a speech may begin with brainstorming. Consider hashing over possible ideas with friends, family, and teachers. Tell them who the audience will be and what your goal or objective is. In a brainstorming session, all parties gathered state their ideas, no matter what comes to mind. Sometimes, a thought that at first seems farfetched can provide the basis for a creative talk. Guide the discussion as it goes along to make sure you get the suggestions you need. Brainstorming is typically a group activity, but individuals can brainstorm on their own as well, jotting down a list of ideas as they come to mind.

With a solid idea for a speech in mind, the presenter can now decide on an approach for writing an effective talk. There are many different possible routes to take to meet this goal.

A terrific speech often starts with some brainstorming. You can spend some time on your own jotting down possible points you'd like to make.

CHRONOLOGICAL ORDER

Information can be organized according to the progression of time. A story can be told from the past to the present and looking to the future. Or it might start from the present and work its way backward. If the topic is the history of anything—flight, Seattle, the Great Wall of China, Pokémon—chronological order can be the best plan of attack. It can also be effective for reviewing how a group formed and continues to this day, whether it be the school French club or a rock band. This approach also works when discussing a person's life as well, whether it's your own or someone else's.

PROBLEM AND SOLUTION

Another strategy is to tell the crowd about a problem that demands their attention. Then provide a solution, outlining how it will be achieved. The audience should be able to visualize how this solution will benefit them and encourage folks to take action to get things done.

A topic might be the lack of healthy food in the school cafeteria and how the kitchen staff can make meals that are more nutritional while not being too expensive and still remain tasty. The answer might be to research recipes online from famous chefs and perhaps get students volunteering in the kitchen to help with the cooking. A variation on the problem and solution tactic is to use a cause-and-effect model. For example, a student may explain before an

Speakers use different techniques to present their information. They may give details in chronological order, pose problems and solutions, or use visual aids.

19

audience that the addition of a new wing to the school can successfully reduce class sizes.

A NUMBERED LIST

Speakers frequently use this tactic. Often a political candidate will rattle off achievements or a plan, giving a number to each item on the list. People seem to have a natural interest in numbered lists. Lists are widely used by top-selling magazines and the Top 10 List was a popular segment on the *Late Show with David Letterman*. A speech may cover the Top Five Reasons School Should Start Later or Six Great Ways to Improve Test Scores.

METAPHORS

Most likely, you've learned about these literary devices in your English class, and what works well in a novel can also make for a memorable speech. These techniques let audiences grasp a concept in an interesting, often visual way.

Metaphors make an implied comparison. A short example: A library is a delivery room for the birth of ideas. A longer metaphor can be found in John Gray's book *The Mars and Venus Diet and Exercise Solution*, in which he compares the body to a steam engine and food to the coal that fuels the engine. When a person does not get the body fires going in the morning with breakfast fuel, the engine slows down and just doesn't operate as well. A student might use

THOSE ARE STRONG WORDS

When crafting a public speech, pay careful attention to word choice. Words matter and can have an impact.

Think about your audience and how some words can be inflammatory or possibly insulting or hurtful. A few carefully selected words can make a difference and help elevate a presentation. Some words are simply more exciting than others, such as "powerful," "pioneering," "game-changing," "triumphant," "jaw-dropping," and "stellar." Gregory Ciotti wrote on the website Copyblogger that these are the most persuasive words in the English language: "you," "free," "because," "instantly," and "new." In his book *Confessions of an Advertising Man,* legendary ad executive David Ogilvy wrote that these are the twenty most influential words: "suddenly," "now," "announcing," "introducing," "improvement," "amazing," "sensational," "remarkable," "revolutionary," "startling," "miracle," "magic," "offer," "quick," "easy," "wanted," "challenge," "compare," "bargain," "hurry." The lesson: choose words wisely and they can have a big impact.

a similar metaphor advocating for more clubs: "Our school is a stew filled with a diverse mix of students. But without some spice, even this rich stew can be bland. The spices that can really bring this stew to life are student organizations."

OTHER TOOLS IN THE KIT

Speechwriters can draw on a number of devices that can make their presentation all the richer. The purpose of most of these tools is to give backup or examples to prove a point.

Quotations, for example, can be a great way to illustrate a point. Famous quotations have gained their status because they are usually very clever and have been uttered by someone who is famous. Here are a few quotes that could possibly kick off a speech:

"The common question that gets asked in business is, 'why?' That's a good question, but an equally valid question is, 'why not?'"—Jeff Bezos

"Eighty percent of success is showing up."—Woody Allen

"Be who you are and say what you feel, because those who mind don't matter and those who matter don't mind."—Dr. Seuss

"There are two ways to live. You can live as if there is no such thing as a miracle, or you can live as if everything is a miracle."—Albert Einstein

To find quotes that match a topic, check online sites such as Bartlett's Familiar Quotations, BrainyQuote, and the Quotations Page.

People love a good story. Personal anecdotes not only keep listeners interested, they also make the speaker more human and relatable. Anecdotes can be about other people as well. Or a short story used to illustrate a point or lesson may be delivered in the form of a fable—fables are all about teaching life lessons. The story of the ant and the grasshopper by the ancient Greek fabulist Aesop is perfect for teaching lessons about the virtues of hard work, planning for the future, and saving. The grasshopper enjoys himself all summer and does no work while the ant works hard to save food for the winter. When winter comes, the ant is prepared while the grasshopper has nothing and goes hungry.

Facts, of course, provide a solid means for backing up points. So it's important to do research. A couple reliable and trusted sources for facts are AmericanFactFinder and Virtual Reference Shelf. Statistics can be especially useful for proving a point. And the numbers can often be eye-opening.

Here are a couple of examples of interesting facts using statistics: In 2013, 10 percent of all drivers ages fifteen to nineteen involved in fatal crashes were reported as distracted at the time of the crash, according to Distraction.gov. On average, Americans eat three hamburgers a week. That's a national total of nearly 50 billion burgers per year, according to a report on the PBS News Hour. A number of websites specialize in providing statistical information, including

Statista, Numberof.net, Knoema, Google Public Data, USA. gov Reference Center, Gallup, and SciVerse. The Guinness Book of World Records is great source for interesting, off-the-wall facts.

In addition, you may research your topic thoroughly, reading books and articles about the subject to be discussed and then referencing them in a speech. To find newspaper and magazine articles, take a look at Google News, Library of Congress, and Newseum. Also, you may reach out directly to experts to interview who can support your message. Getting direct quotes from knowledgeable sources can make a speech truly original.

OVERALL TIPS

With all research complete and a basic organizational approach in mind, you can begin to write the speech. Creating an outline often helps. Consider length as well. This will often depend on the amount of material that must be covered and any time limits given. The organizers of TED Talks have studied public speaking a great deal, and they concluded that the ideal length of a presentation is eighteen minutes—a segment of time during which most people can pay attention before they tune out.

Decide on the introduction. It needs to grab the audience's interest. It might also have to include who you are if listeners don't already know. Then sketch out the information that must be included and how the presentation will flow. The conclusion should be memorable as well and leave the listeners with a summation of the main ideas and often a call for action—what needs to be done next? To keep the whole speech lively, mix in different elements—stories, facts, opinions, etc. You may want to engage the audience by asking a question and being ready to address the answers. Or you might ask attendees if they have any questions.

Peter Jeff, who wrote the article "10 Ways to End Your Speech with a Bang," advises ending with "an attitude not a platitude." He suggests leaving the crowd with final passionate thoughts that will galvanize the audience. The eighteenth-century politician Patrick Henry

With a little research, you can find statistics, quotes, and other information to make a presentation more credible.

did just such a thing when he ended his speech of March 23, 1775, calling Virginia to form militias to defend itself against the British: "Is life so dear or peace so sweet as to be purchased at the price of chains and slavery. Forbid it, Almighty God! I know not what course others may take but as for me give me liberty or give me death."

Practice Makes Perfect

Getting a speech down on paper is only half the battle. The next part is being able to deliver it. Your words may be perfect on the page, but they won't have their intended punch if you can't speak with flow, clarity, and conviction.

As lifelong politician Hillary Clinton said in an interview in *Glamour* magazine, "If you're not comfortable with public speaking—and nobody starts out comfortable; you have to learn how to be comfortable—practice. I cannot overstate the importance of practicing. Get some close friends or family members to help evaluate you, or somebody at work that you trust."

REHEARSE UNTIL YOU DROP

Clinton has made thousands of speeches and knows that practice pays off. The more you rehearse, the better you get. How much time should you put in? Nancy Duarte, the author of *slide:ology The Art and Science of Creating Great*

How do you make a smooth, forceful presentation without stumbling or awkward pauses? The answer is: practice.

Presentations, suggests that an individual spend thirty-six to ninety hours preparing for a one-hour presentation—certainly a great length of time. Scott Schwertly, author of *How to Be a Presentation God*, recommends practicing a speech seven to eight times.

Once your speech is written, read it aloud. You don't need anyone to hear you read at first—just listen to how it sounds to yourself as you read it. By reading a speech aloud, the presenter can hear what parts are working and what sections may need additional work. Think about pace. Is the talk rushing or moving along slowly with fits and starts? Does it build? Does it have some drama?

Be sure to check its length. Is the presentation running too long or too short? It may either need some cutting back or some additional material. Be aware if certain passages leave you stumbling verbally or tongue-tied. Certain combinations of words are simply hard to say. Rework any of those passages and smooth things out.

BE YOUR OWN AUDIENCE

Videotaping your presentation can help as well. By reviewing a taped performance, you can be more critical. Are you too stiff? Are you monotone? Think about tone and projecting your voice. The voice can be stronger when emphasizing matters, but pull back for quieter moments. Vocal dynamics make a more textured performance.

Try giving the talk in front of the mirror. It helps give a sense of how you will appear before the audience. Think if you're projecting enough so your voice can be heard. Check posture—standing up straight communicates confidence while slouching can make a bad impression. There can be a tendency to rush. Take deep breaths and leave room for pauses.

Although a presentation may seem to be going slow in a speaker's mind, that is often not the case for the audience. Plus, an audience that has to follow a speaker who is changing position is more likely to stay awake. A dramatic pause can be taken by going silent, walking a few steps deep in thought, then looking up and putting forth a tremendous insight. Also, consider doing a dress rehearsal in the clothes you intend to wear so that you will be accustomed to the exact outfit come showtime.

Kyle Pott of Lifehacker.com advises rehearsing to a wall as well. He writes: "Speaking in front of a wall will

Videotaping a practice round of a speech can help a presenter evaluate what's working and what isn't.

allow you to block out all distractions and focus exclusively on the content of your speech. You may feel silly doing this at first (I certainly did) but speaking in front of a wall will help you identify the parts of your speech that you are struggling with, in which the content is weak, or that you cannot gracefully convey to your audience."

MOVE AROUND!

In the past, public speaking experts recommended standing perfectly still behind a podium. But that philosophy has changed. There's nothing wrong with that style, but speaking and moving shows a person is dynamic. The motion provides an element of entertainment and communicates confidence and comfort.

While it can be fine to have notes or the actual script in front of you, reading a speech directly off the page does

THREE SPEAKING TICS AND HOW TO STOP THEM

- **Stop Saying Filler Words.** Many of us fill up pauses in speech with repetitive and frequently annoying words that are unnecessary: "you know," "like," "anyway," "right?" "well," and "so." These can all be overused and can make a talk more annoying and tedious. Listen to a tape so you can be aware of how much you utter these words and then make a conscious effort to say nothing where you would normally spit out some filler. Remember, people need pauses to process information so don't worry about short silences.

- **Lose a Scratchy Throat.** A rough sounding voice, loud sniffing, or a persistent cough can kill a presentation. Make sure you have water. Beforehand, relax and clear the throat as much as possible. Give a forceful pitch but not to a fevered pitch where you might blow out your voice.

- **Don't Sound Cold and Robotic.** There can be a tendency to communicate in a stiff, almost academic way that gives information but doesn't connect on a human level with the audience. That can make a speaker seems distant. Again, know your audience. A speech that is "too smart" may not connect. Remember to keep it warm and friendly.

not capture interest like one that is conveyed from memory. A memorized talk becomes more of a performance. An audience will be more captivated if you look at them, than if they have to watch the top of your head as you look down at a script. Sometimes, holding a few note cards can be a less obtrusive crutch, rather than shuffling through a stack of sheets.

People who are new to public speaking may wonder where to look when facing the crowd. Alex Rister on the website Six Minutes: Speaking and Presentation Skills: Your Guide to Be a Confident and Effective Speaker says that making eye contact with audience members is important because it conveys that you are delivering a message directly to them. In *Inc.* magazine, Sims Wyeth, a professional development and executive presence coach, writes that eye contact makes the talker more authoritative, confident, and believable. Listeners become more actively engaged rather than passively taking in the speech. Eye contact helps build empathy. Still, there has to be a balance to offer some relief. Too much staring at a person in the audience can be unnerving.

Hand gestures are another way to keep folks engaged. ScienceofPeople.com analyzed thousands of hours of TED Talks and found one striking pattern: The most viral talkers communicated with their hands. Gestures help others remember what the speaker says, and they help the speaker remember as well. Experts emphasize, however, not to

You can enhance your speech with hand gestures. The right motions can captivate, while some gestures can send a negative vibe.

overdo gestures. Too much and a lecturer appears to be flailing around.

A recommended zone for gesturing is from the top of the chest to the bottom of the waist. Do not talk with your arms folded—this sends a signal of being unreceptive. If you have any props or other visuals, go over how you will use them. Bringing props into the picture can take a little extra coordination as far as when and how to pick them up and present them to the audience. That's why it's key to practice with any visual aids you intend on using.

FIND A TEST AUDIENCE

Once you think you have thoroughly rehearsed on your own, gather your test subjects—friends, family, teachers, coworkers—whomever you trust to give honest feedback. Some say it is wise to rehearse before non-friends because they will be more honest in their critique. A pet may even prove useful. At American University's Kogod School of Business, students can sharpen their public speaking skills in front of nonjudgmental "audience dogs." The school says that practicing before a canine can lower blood pressure, decrease stress, and elevate mood.

When speaking to a human practice audience, give them criteria by which to judge you. How many times did you say "umm" or "errr" or "like" or other annoying filler words? Ask if you had any irritating mannerisms, such as playing with a ring or pen, or jangling change in a pocket. For your dry run, attempt to make it as close to the actual performance as possible—use the same gestures, try to duplicate the lighting, wear the same clothes. Don't come in a T-shirt and cut-offs if you'll be wearing a suit and tie at the presentation.

Almost everyone gets nervous to some degree performing before a crowd. Nothing creates more nervousness than not being prepared. When a person has the words firmly ingrained in his or her memory, they flow out and it is less likely the person will make a mistake or lose his or her place.

Presenting a talk before a test audience will make giving the actual speech much easier, and your sample crowd can provide feedback on strengths and weaknesses.

CHAPTER FOUR

The Moment Has Arrived

When the day to give a speech arrives, make sure you are ready. Be well rested and well fed. Being too tired or hungry has the potential to ruin any performance. Take a look at yourself in the mirror. Are you looking neat and clean? Are your clothes free of lint and small stains? You want to look sharp and professional. Double check you have all the notes you need, as well as any props, charts, and visuals.

A speaker usually wants access to the space prior to the event. This allows the presenter a chance to picture the environment he or she will be working in. If using a microphone, sound system, and lighting, he or she will want to test everything out and if there is enough time, do an entire run-through. In situations where the seats are moveable, such as a classroom, these may be arranged beforehand to give the best sightlines for the audience.

Seats may have to be pushed back to make room for talking and a bit of walking. If there's a small group of listeners, consider arranging chairs in a semicircle. Also, if someone is available to help, have that person stand where you will speak and take a seat in the audience. Make sure that everything looks right from the audience perspective. Remove or cover anything in the room that might prove to be a distraction. This could mean closing the blinds as well.

PREPPING VISUALS AIDS

The use of photographs, graphs, pictures, diagrams, sketches, and other visual aids can pump up any presentation. In general, they help grab viewers' attention and help them understand and remember information. All visuals need to

Before the actual speech begins, a presenter will want to make sure all equipment is operating correctly.

be big enough for the audience to see, and presenters need to practice where to stand so they do not block any views. One tip, however: never turn your back on the audience.

Instead of bringing physical large charts on poster board or any other physical props, many visuals can be easily projected from electronic files. With the right audio cable and video cable (usually VGA or video graphics array), a laptop can be connected to a projector or audiovisual system in a theater. Most laptops also support HDMI connections. Short for high definition multimedia interface, HDMI is a connector and cable capable of transmitting high-quality and high-bandwidth streams of audio and video between devices. The image on the computer screen will show up on the big screen via the projector.

With this connection, you can show videos, slideshows, jpegs, or PDFs of charts and documents. When bringing a laptop, review that all files are in place and that you've brought along the necessary power cords. (Sometimes it's wise to carry an extension cord and three-prong adapter as well.) You might also bring the visual presentation on a USB drive or DVD, depending on the setup, and then project them through available equipment. If the system has WiFi access, certain items might be viewable direct from the internet.

There are several types of software and platforms that are designed to make presentations. These are vehicles to help tell a story. PowerPoint is perhaps the best of them all,

Visuals can bring vitality and punch. Many conference rooms and auditoriums are already equipped to project videos and still images from a computer.

having been around for just over twenty-five years. Other popular presentation platforms include Keynote and Prezi. These tools simplify the process for making graphics. For example, a flat, lifeless list of bulleted items can be jazzed up with functions that convert them into eye-popping graphics. These software programs also give options to display numerical data in various visual ways. Even simple animations can be created.

It's crucial to test any electronic media like this works properly and that the speaker will be able to operate the equipment or have someone else operate the equipment while he or she is talking. Some other presentation programs are CustomShow, ClearSlide, SlideShark, Haiku Deck, PowToon, and Knowledge Vision.

DEALING WITH STAGE FRIGHT

Although you may have all the elements prepared for a perfect speech, one more hurdle may block you from giving a stellar performance: stage fright. While almost everyone gets a little nervous before going on stage, this condition is an extreme case of anxiety. The afflicted are overcome by dread and panic. Although some people try natural remedies or therapy to reduce their performance anxiety, there are techniques that a person can try to empower themselves, build confidence, and beat back the feelings of fear. The Anxiety and Depression Association of America advises trying these tips to decrease stage fright.

- Shift the focus from yourself and your fear to your true purpose—contributing something of value to your audience.

- Stop scaring yourself with thoughts about what might go wrong. Instead, focus your attention on thoughts and images that are calming and reassuring.

- Refuse to think thoughts that create self-doubt and low confidence.

- Practice ways to relax your mind and body, such as deep breathing, relaxation exercises, yoga, and meditation.

- Exercise, eat well, and practice other healthful life-style habits. Try to limit caffeine, and sugar as much as possible.

- Visualize your success: always focus on your strength and ability to handle challenging situations.

- Prepare your material in advance and read it aloud to hear your voice. Make connections with your audience. Smile and greet people, thinking of them as friends rather than enemies.

- Stand or sit in a self-assured, confident posture. Remain warm and open and make eye contact.

- Give up trying to be perfect and know that it is OK to make mistakes. Be natural, be yourself.

Often if you can successfully get through the first few minutes of your speech, you will start to adjust to the situation and anxiety will decrease. Also, remember that you are your own worst critic—people aren't coming to pick you apart. In general, people will be supportive—they want to see you succeed. If nerves start to get to you and you wobble, don't be afraid to take a pause. Take those deep breaths and maybe a sip of water. Consider not holding your notes in front of you because the audience will see the notes shaking. If you can, get behind a podium or desk where you can set down notes and even steady yourself against the furniture.

EVEN CELEBRITIES GET STAGE FRIGHT

If you have experienced stage fright, you are not alone. There are many famous people who regularly get in the spotlight but who have also suffered from stage fright along the way. Singer Barbra Streisand may be one of the most known cases. After suffering a panic attack during a 1967 concert in Central Park when she forgot the lyrics, she avoided live performances for decades. Streisand returned to that stage in the 1990s, controlling her anxiety with medication and teleprompters.

Carly Simon has had such bad stage fright that she even passed out on stage once. The American opera singer Renée Fleming suffered such performance anxiety that her vocal coach had to push her out on the stage. "We're talking about deep, deep panic, and that every fiber of your being is saying, 'I cannot be on that stage,'" said Fleming in an article on CBSNews.com.

At age fifteen, the comedian Jim Carrey had such a horrible performing experience that he almost never returned to the stage. He bombed at a comedy club where the audience put him down and the host called him "boring." It took him two years to get over the trauma and try again.

The singer Adele says she has stage fright because she doesn't want to let fans down. When musician André 3000 performed at the outdoor music fest Coachella, he was overcome with anxiety, a problem he has often struggled with. Because singer Fiona Apple stressed so much over how she was perceived on stage, she took several years off from live performing. Taking a break helped her relax. When she returned, she said that performing didn't feel like such a life-and-death matter any more.

WHEN YOU'RE IN THE DANCE

Before you take the stage, you should find a mirror and take one last look at yourself. Once you've overcome any initial nerves and your speech is under way, be aware of your delivery. Be upbeat and smile. Be sure you are projecting your voice or speaking into the microphone so all your words are being heard. Keep up the eye contact. Be enthusiastic, and don't let your energy flag. At the same time, don't be too manic or overwhelming. If you fumble a line, don't sweat it. You might correct yourself, but just move on. Be ready for anything.

If the microphone cuts out, step foward and tell the audience what's going on and try to continue by speaking loudly to the crowd.

CHAPTER FIVE

A Tool for Advancement

Having great public speaking skills can give you a great advantage in life. When you get good at public speaking, it makes you a more competitive employee. Public speaking is one of the main tools of leadership because you can gather people together in one room and deliver a message that will have a higher likelihood of moving them to action. This is a skill that bosses want— it makes you more visible and valuable and therefore indispensible. The skill can help earn a promotion and it can translate to almost any field.

Giving a speech can better clarify your role and mission as well. It can be a great way to connect with new people and network for future possible jobs. As a powerful public speaker, you can be the driver of positive change. A great talk can make a long-lasting positive impression, and by the same token, a bad presentation can leave a crowd doubting your capabilities. But remember, if a speech doesn't go over so well, failure can actually pave the way to success. Learn from your mistakes, improve, and try again.

Whether it be through speaking to crowds or to small groups, an effective, organized presenter can become a leader in almost any organization.

Winston Churchill fainted at his first speech before Parliament, and Bill Clinton was booed for his long-windedness at the Democratic convention in 1988. Becoming a solid speechmaker takes practice.

GOOD SPEAKERS WANTED

A recent survey from Prezi (a presentation software company) and Harris Polls found that 70 percent of employed Americans who give presentations believe presentation skills are critical for career success. Three out of four wish they were better at it. In the same study, however, two out of ten respondents said that they would do almost anything to avoid giving a public talk, including faking illness or asking a coworker to give the presentation.

For employers, good presentation skills also indicate sharp critical-thinking skills. In preparing a speech, you're often considering real problems and effective possible solutions. The ability to think through these matters and consider potential costs and benefits are of great value to businesses. This process requires conducting and analyzing research—another talent that companies highly value.

Polished speech-making skills can pave the way to success in the workplace. Employers value those who use their words to motivate and convey what needs to get done.

A PATH TOWARD LEADERSHIP

Those who become very good at public speaking find themselves building a name for themselves and climbing the corporate ladder. Promotions are directly linked to an ability to communicate effectively. As the ability to speak well before others grows, so does overall confidence.

The smooth communicators can become the face of a company. They are the ones who get to have the most client contact, and that can lead to earning more money. In *Forbes* magazine, the writer Carmine Gallo said that he regularly receives emails from readers who have shared how their communication skills have led to success. One such example is a mid-level manager who swiftly climbed the ranks of his Fortune 500 technology firm because he was considered one of the company's best presenters. Another example is a marketing manager of a large construction firm who re-tooled the company's PowerPoint presentation and landed an $875 million contract.

Great speakers know how to successfully pitch a new product idea or present a financial analysis or strategic plan to a management team. Bill Driscoll is the New England district president of Accountemps, a staffing agency for accounting, finance, and bookkeeping professionals. He said in an article titled "Employers Say Verbal Communication Is the Most Important Skill for Job Candidates, Reveals New Report" that verbal communication skills are crucial to explaining the meaning behind business decisions to a variety of audiences.

For those still in school, these talents make students shine in the classroom as well. After all, teaching is all about standing before a crowd and providing entertainment, hopefully in a riveting manner. Gallo has also written about how billionaire Warren Buffet believes that public speaking skills raise an employee's value by 50 percent.

While these verbal talents can elevate any employee, the personal finances and career website The Balance says that these skills are central to certain jobs in particular: consultants, trainers, sales representatives, actors, motivational speakers, broadcasters, public relations representatives, recruiters, public officials, managers, clergy, attorneys, association leaders, admissions representatives, fundraisers, and teachers.

The great added benefit to honing communication ability is that the talent carries over to other parts of a job. Phone sales, conversations with colleagues and mentors, and more general everyday interactions may improve. When a person communicates with others more clearly, mistakes are avoided and tasks and goals can be completed more efficiently. They can become so respected in their fields that they become "thought leaders." Joel Kurtzman, the editor of *strategy + business* magazine, coined the phrase "thought leaders" to describe professionals who become authorities on a subject and contribute new ideas to the business world. (He used the term in the first issue of *strategy + business*.)

By sharpening public speaking skills, all professional communications can improve, including interactions with the boss, conference room meetings, and sales calls.

Because thought leaders are so highly sought after and have highly regarded "intellectual capital," they earn more money.

So if you're a job seeker, you will want to include public speaking experience in your résumé or a sample in your portfolio. If you maintain a website regarding your work life, you could feature video clips of you giving a presentation.

As young people embark on their career journey, they should look to the thought leaders in their field. Analyze their speeches and think about what technique and subjects have made them so successful. Some powerhouse thought leaders are Jay Baer in the world of marketing (he runs a

CONNECT TO HELPFUL SOURCES

There are many online resources for improving public speaking skills. Here are a few of the best:

- **SlideShare.** On this site, users share what they know and love through presentations, infographics, documents, and more.

- **Giving an Academic Talk**. This web page by Jonathan Sewchuk, a professor of computer science at the University of California at Berkeley, gives advice on how to give a presentation in an academic setting.

- **Everything I Know About Presentations I Learned in Theatre School**. This blog post by Darren Barefoot highlights how getting involved in theater can really help a student build public speaking skills.

- **Toastmasters International.** Since 1924, this organization has been a respected authority on how to give public talks. The site offers helpful advice, as well as an entertaining podcast.

- **MIT: Public Speaking Tips.** On this web page on the MIT website, researchers at the famous science and technology school cover many interesting aspects of speech making, from the sound of the voice to mapping the content for a public speech.

blog called Convince & Convert), Amy Edmondson (a Harvard Business School professor and leadership expert), and Richard Florida (who researches the growing importance of creative types across all industries).

THE IMPROMPTU SPEECH

As you become more comfortable speaking in front of an audience, you may be able to give an impromptu speech. The occasion often comes up. Someone drops out and a replacement is needed. Or people call for a speech at a wedding, birthday, or other special occasion. If you have at least a few

When you get good at speaking in front of others, you can make a speech without even preparing. This can come in handy at social functions, such as weddings.

minutes, you might grab a napkin or piece of paper and jot down a few thoughts. Try to think of a great opening line—once you break the ice with an opener, it can often be easier to go on. If time permits, write down a closing thought as well so things will wrap up nicely. Sometimes, you might have an anecdote or story or points from a previous speech that worked nicely—think if you can reuse anything from a past presentation. If you need a moment to think, consider asking the crowd a question—Any questions? What was your wedding like?

Opportunities to give speeches often come up—take advantage of them. As Sims Wyeth writes in his book *The Essentials of Persuasive Public Speaking*, quality comes from quantity. The more you do, the better you get. If you're still in school, there are many situations that can give practice. Look into joining extracurricular groups. Drama club, debate club, and student government, for example, offer the chance to hone presentation skills. Whatever you do, don't rule yourself out when it comes to public speaking. It is a talent that you can become good at. In time, you may find a voice that is uniquely you—and that will be welcomed. As the billionaire entrepreneur and founder of Virgin Atlantic airline, Richard Branson, once said, "Communication is an important skill any leader can possess."

GLOSSARY

ANECDOTE A short, usually amusing account of a particular incident or event.

AUTHORITATIVE Having or displaying impressive knowledge about a subject.

BRAINSTORM To come up with a lot of ideas very quickly for a future project before considering some of them more carefully.

DISCRIMINATION The practice of unfairly treating a person or group of people differently from other people or groups of people.

DRY RUN A rehearsal of a performance before the actual performance.

ENGAGE To involve or attract someone's interest or attention.

GALVANIZE To excite someone to take action.

GLOSSOPHOBIA The fear of public speaking.

IMPROMPTU Unrehearsed, unprepared, unscripted action.

INDISPENSABLE Absolutely necessary.

JPEG A format for compressing digital image files.

MANNERISM A habitual way of moving, gesturing,

speaking, or behaving.

METAPHOR A word or phrase for one thing that is used to refer to another thing to indicate that they are similar.

OBJECTIVE Something that one's efforts are intended to accomplish.

PDF A file format that provides an electronic image of text or text and graphics.

PERSUASIVE Convincing.

PODIUM A stand for holding the notes of a public speaker; also called a lectern.

PROJECT To use the voice loudly, strongly, and clearly.

PROMOTION An advancement of an employee within a company.

RATIONALE Reason behind a plan, belief, action, or decision.

STATISTICS The science of collecting, analyzing, and interpreting masses of numerical data.

USB DRIVE An external flash drive that can be used with a USB (universal serial bus) port on a computer.

FOR MORE INFORMATION

Canadian Association of Professional Speakers (CAPS)
1370 Don Mills Road, Suite 300
Toronto, ON M3B 3N7
Canada
(877) 847-3350
Website: http://www.canadianspeakers.org
This resource for those who speak professionally offers
information and networking for those who talk in
public.

National Speakers Association
1500 South Priest Drive
Tempe, AZ 85281
(480) 968-2552
Website: http://www.nsaspeaker.org
This organization provides resources and education
designed to advance the speaking profession. The
NSA offers student memberships.

Public Speakers Association
PO Box 181
Cedar Park, TX 78630
(512) 456-7163
Website: http://www.publicspeakersassociation.com
With the motto "Change the World from the Front of the
Room," this association provides resources and edu-
cational materials from those making presentations.

The Rotary Foundation
c/o 911600
PO Box 4090 STN A
Toronto, ON M5W 0E9
(866) 976-8279
Website: https://www.rotary.org
This Canadian foundation has a mission to advance world
understanding, goodwill, and peace through the
improvement of health, the support of education, and
the alleviation of poverty. The group promotes public
speaking among its members.

Toastmasters International
PO Box 9052
Mission Viejo, CA 92690-9052
(949) 858-8255
Website: http://www.toastmasters.org
This nonprofit educational group is dedicated to teaching
public speaking and leadership.

WEBSITES

Because of the changing nature of internet links, Rosen
Publishing has developed an online list of websites related
to the subject of this book. This site is updated regularly.
Please use this link to access the list:

http://www.rosenlinks.com/SFS/public

FOR FURTHER READING

Anderson, Chris. *TED Talks: The Official TED Guide to Public Speaking.* New York: NY: Houghton Mifflin Harcourt, 2016.

Beebe, Steven, and Susan Beebe. *Public Speaking: An Audience-Centered Approach.* New York, NY: Pearson, 2014.

Carnegie, Dale. *Public Speaking for Success: The Complete Program, Revised and Updated.* New York, NY: Penguin, 2006.

Fraleigh, Douglas, and Joseph Tuman. *Speak Up! An Illustrated Guide to Public Speaking.* 3rd Edition. New York: NY: Bedford/St. Martin's, 2014.

Lucas, Stephen. *The Art of Public Speaking.* New York: NY: McGraw-Hill Education, 2014.

Port, Michael. *Steal the Show: From Speeches to Job Interviews to Deal-Closing Pitches, How to Guarantee a Standing Ovation for All the Performances in Your Life.* New York: NY: Houghton Mifflin Harcourt, 2015.

Rothwell, J. Dan. *Practically Speaking.* New York, NY: Oxford University Press, 2013.

Wyeth, Sims. *The Essentials of Persuasive Public Speaking.* New York, NY: W.W. Norton, 2014.

BIBLIOGRAPHY

Adams, Susan. "4 Steps to Successful Brainstorming." *Forbes*. March 5, 2013. http://www.forbes.com.

Boundless. "Types of Informative Speeches." Boundless Communications. September 20, 2016. https://www.boundless.com.

Boy Scouts of America. *Public Speaking*. Irving, TX: Boy Scouts of America, 2011.

Concordia University. "Simple Steps to Create a Persuasive Speech." September 29, 2012. http://education.cu-portland.edu/blog/educator-tips/simple-steps-to-create-a-persuasive-speech-lesson-plan.

Doyle, Allison. "Public Speaking Skills to Include in Your Resume." The Balance. July 20, 2016. https://www.thebalance.com/public-speaking-skills-with-examples-2059697.

Esposito, Janet. "Conquering Stage Fright." Anxiety and Depression Association of America. Retrieved October 15, 2016. https://www.adaa.org/understanding-anxiety/social-anxiety-disorder/treatment/conquering-stage-fright.

Fleming, Grace. "Impromptu Speech with Little or No Time to Prepare." AboutEducation. July 17, 2016. http://homeworktips.about.com/od/speechclass/a/impromptu.htm.

Gallo, Carmine. "New Survey: 70% Say Presentation Skills Are Critical for Career Success." *Forbes*. September 25, 2014. http://www.forbes.com.

Gallo, Carmine. "One Skill That Will Boost Your Value by Fifty Percent." *Forbes*. December 27, 2013. http://www.forbes.com.

GMAT. "Employers Want Communications Skills in New Hires." August 7, 2014. http://www.mba.com.

Hollis, Billy. "Top Five Public Speaking Tics That Are Annoying as Hell." Questions and Observations. August 28, 2011. http://www.qando.net.

Mason, Emma. "Is Martin Luther King's 'I Have a Dream' the Greatest Speech in History?" HistoryExtra. January 15, 2016. http://www.historyextra.com/feature/martin-luther-kings-i-have-dream-greatest-speech-history.

New York Film Academy. "Stage Fright: Examples & Lessons From Famous Sufferers." July 1, 2014. https://www.nyfa.edu/student-resources/stage-fright-examples-lessons-famous-sufferers.

Persuasive Speech Topics and Ideas. "The Master Orators: Famous Persuasive Speeches." Retrieved October 15, 2016. http://persuasivespeechideas.org/famous-persuasive-speeches.

Statz, Sarah R. *Public Speaking Handbook for Librarians and Information Professionals.* Jefferson, NC: McFarland & Company, 2003.

TeachingAmericanHistory.org. "FDR Speaks to a Nation in Crisis, March 4, 1933." March 4, 2013. http://teachingamericanhistory.org/newsletter/201303-2.

University of Pittsburgh. "Persuasive Speaking." August 21, 2008. http://www.speaking.pitt.edu/student/public-speaking/persuasive.html

UShistory.org. "Ask Not What You Can Do for Your Country." Retrieved October 15, 2016. http://www.ushistory.org/documents/ask-not.htm.

Wrench, Jason, Anne Goding, et al. "Why Public Speaking Matters Today." Retrieved October 15, 2016. http://2012books.lardbucket.org/books/public-speaking-practice-and-ethics/s04-why-public-speaking-matters-to.html.

Wyeth, Sims. *The Essentials of Persuasive Public Speaking.* New York, NY: W.W. Norton, 2014.

INDEX

ABOUT THE AUTHOR

Don Rauf is the author of many nonfiction books for young people, including *Kickstarter, Killer Lipstick and Other Spy Gadgets, Virtual Reality, Getting the Most Out of Makerspaces to Explore Arduino & Electronics, Getting the Most Out of Makerspaces to Build Unmanned Aerial Vehicles,* and *Powering Up a Career in Internet Security.*

PHOTO CREDITS